Makers as INNOVATORS JUNIOR

Controlling an Ozobot

By Amber Lovett

Published in the United States of America by
Cherry Lake Publishing
Ann Arbor, Michigan
www.cherrylakepublishing.com

Series Adviser: Kristin Fontichiaro
Reading Adviser: Marla Conn, MS, Ed., Literacy specialist, Read-Ability, Inc.
Photo Credits: All photos by Amber Lovett

Library of Congress Cataloging-in-Publication Data
Names: Lovett, Amber, author.
Title: Controlling an Ozobot / by Amber Lovett.
Other titles: 21st century skills innovation library. Makers as innovators.
Description: Ann Arbor, Michigan : Cherry Lake Publishing, [2017] | Series: Makers as innovators junior | Series: 21st century skills innovation library | Audience: K to grade 3. | Includes bibliographical references and index.
Identifiers: LCCN 2016032415| ISBN 9781634721875 (lib. bdg.) | ISBN 9781634723190 (pbk.) | ISBN 9781634722537 (pdf) | ISBN 9781634723855 (ebook)
Subjects: LCSH: Robots–Juvenile literature. | Robots–Programming–Juvenile literature. | Personal robotics–Juvenile literature.
Classification: LCC TJ211.2 .L68 2017 | DDC 629.8/92–dc23 LC record available at https://lccn.loc.gov/2016032415

Cherry Lake Publishing would like to acknowledge the work of the Partnership for 21st Century Learning. Please visit *www.p21.org* for more information.

Printed in the United States of America
Corporate Graphics

A Note to Adults: Please review the instructions for the activities in this book before allowing children to do them. Be sure to help them with any activities you do not think they can safely complete on their own.

A Note to Kids: Be sure to ask an adult for help with these activities when you need it. Always put your safety first!

Table of Contents

Ozobot 1.0 is black, and Ozobot Bit is clear.

What Is an Ozobot?

Ozobot is a robot. It moves on two wheels. It can also spin and flash its lights. The most special thing about Ozobot is that it can see. Ozobot uses its **sensors** to see the colors red, green, blue, and black. This lets Ozobot follow paths drawn in these colors.

What Can I Do with Ozobot?

You can control Ozobot by drawing paths for it on paper. You can also control Ozobot with a computer. Ozobot can help you learn more about how computers work by using **code**.

Ozobot Bit can follow paths drawn on a tablet with the Ozobot app.

Types of Ozobots

There are two kinds of Ozobots. The first is called Ozobot 1.0. Ozobot 1.0 can follow the lines you draw for it. It can also read special codes called **OzoCodes**. The second kind of Ozobot is the Ozobot Bit. This Ozobot can do everything Ozobot 1.0 does. It can also be controlled using a computer or tablet.

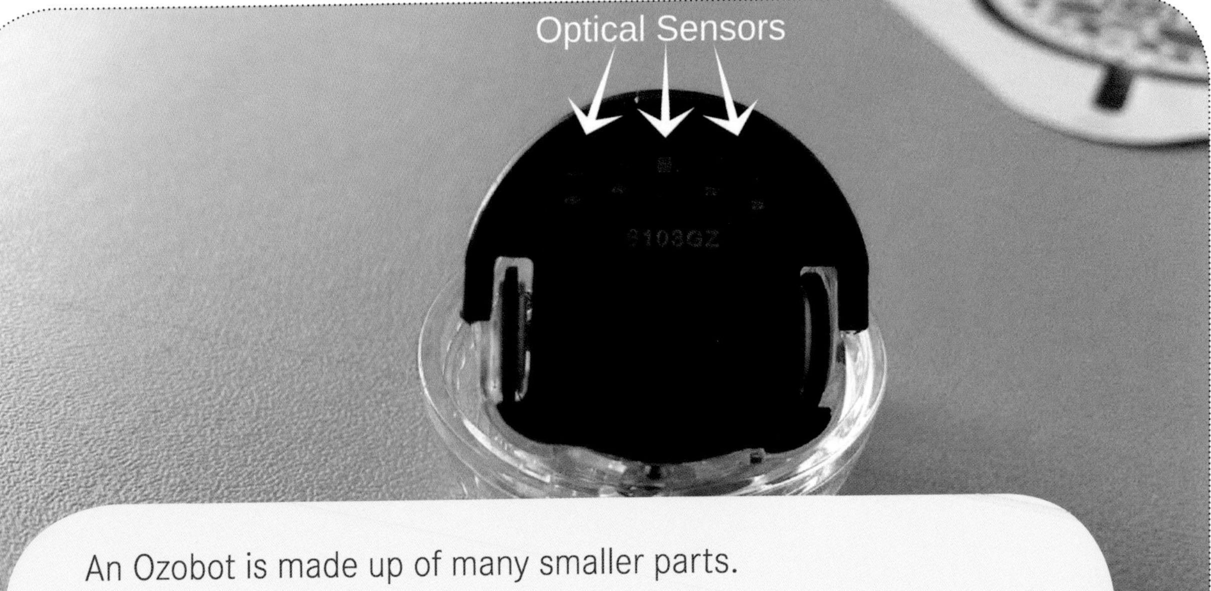

An Ozobot is made up of many smaller parts.

What Are the Parts of an Ozobot?

Outside Ozobot

- Main board: The main board is a tiny computer. It is the Ozobot's brain.
- Sensors: Ozobot's **optical** sensors are like its eyes. They see light and follow your paths.
- Power button: This button turns Ozobot on and off.

Inside Ozobot

- Battery: The battery powers Ozobot.
- Motors: Motors make Ozobot's wheels turn.

Ozobot's light will turn from blue to white when it is ready to calibrate.

Starting with Ozobot

It's a good idea to **calibrate** your Ozobot when you use it on a new kind of paper.

1. Draw a black circle on the paper you are going to use.
2. Hold down Ozobot's power button. The lights will blink.
3. Put Ozobot on the circle.
4. Ozobot will drive to the edge of the circle. Its lights will flash green.

You can use Ozobot with Ozocards like the ones in this picture.

Drawing Paths

Ozobot comes with special cards called Ozocards. They have paths printed on them that Ozobot can follow. You can also draw your own paths for Ozobot using markers. You can use regular markers or permanent markers. Remember, the only colors Ozobot can see are red, blue, green, and black!

Making your turns curved like the box on the right will make it easier for Ozobot to follow your path.

Adding Turns

You can add turns to your path. It is easier for Ozobot to follow curved turns. Sharp turns are harder to follow. It is a lot of fun to watch Ozobot follow a complicated path! Try taping several pieces of paper together to draw longer paths for Ozobot. You can also use big rolls of paper.

Can you figure out what these OzoCodes do? Try re-creating them with your Ozobot and see what happens! What happens if you change the direction Ozobot is going?

What Are OzoCodes?

OzoCodes are combinations of colored blocks. They give Ozobot special instructions. When you use an OzoCode in your path, the Ozobot reads it. Try using the codes below. You can find all of the OzoCodes at *www.ozobot.com.*

Programming Ozobot

If you have an Ozobot Bit, you can do even more. You can write special **programs** for your Ozobot using OzoBlockly. To use OzoBlockly, ask an adult to visit *www.ozoblockly.com* with you. Next, you will drag and arrange colored blocks. It is kind of like creating your own OzoCodes!

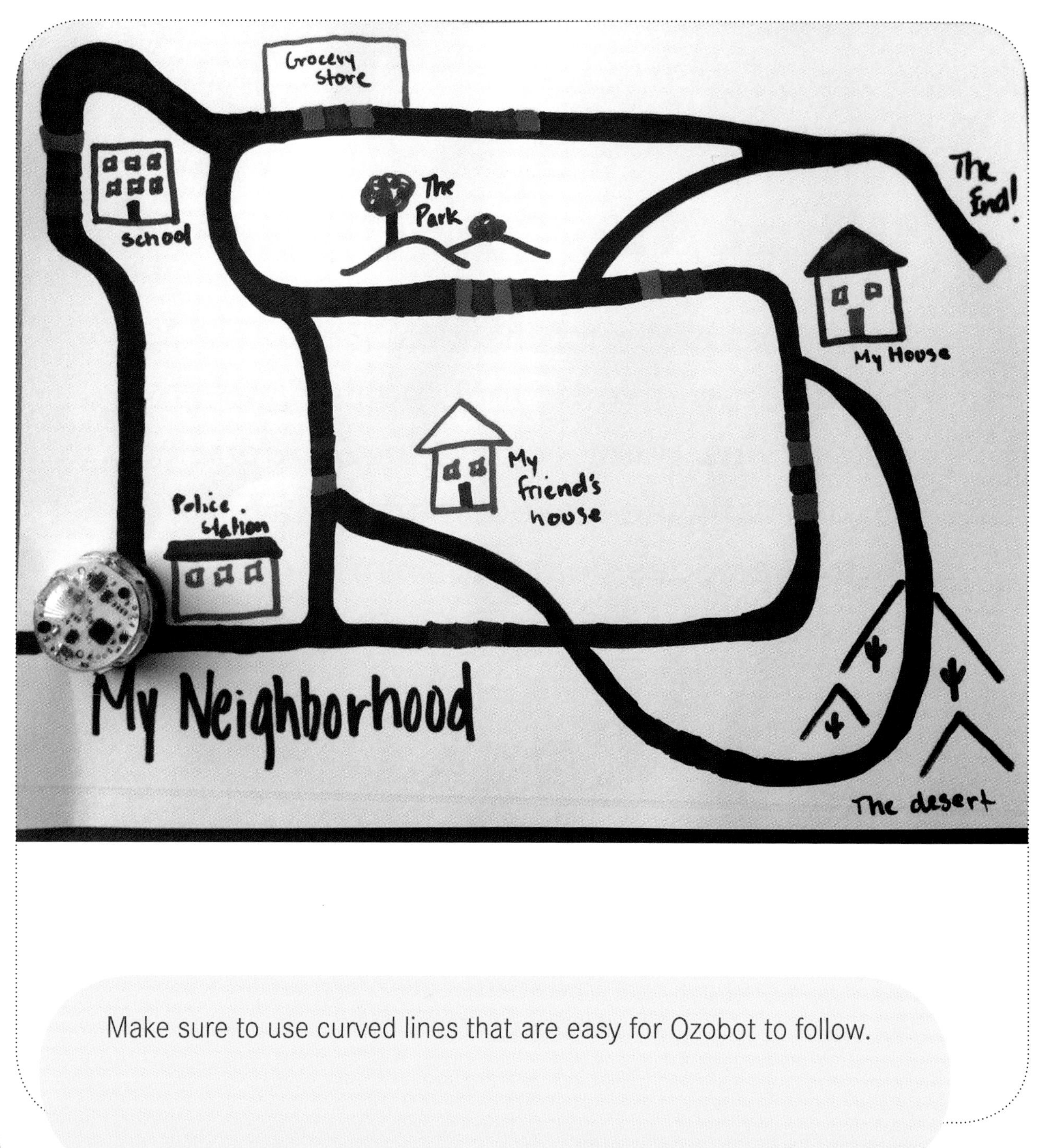

Make sure to use curved lines that are easy for Ozobot to follow.

Your Neighborhood

Show Ozobot around your neighborhood! Use black, red, blue, and green markers to draw a map of your neighborhood on white paper. Make sure the map has a path for Ozobot to follow. You can make your path more complicated by adding forks and turns.

What Is in Your Neighborhood?

Mark important locations on your neighborhood map. Here are some places you might include:

- Your house
- Your school
- Friends' houses
- Parks and playgrounds
- Stores you visit
- The library

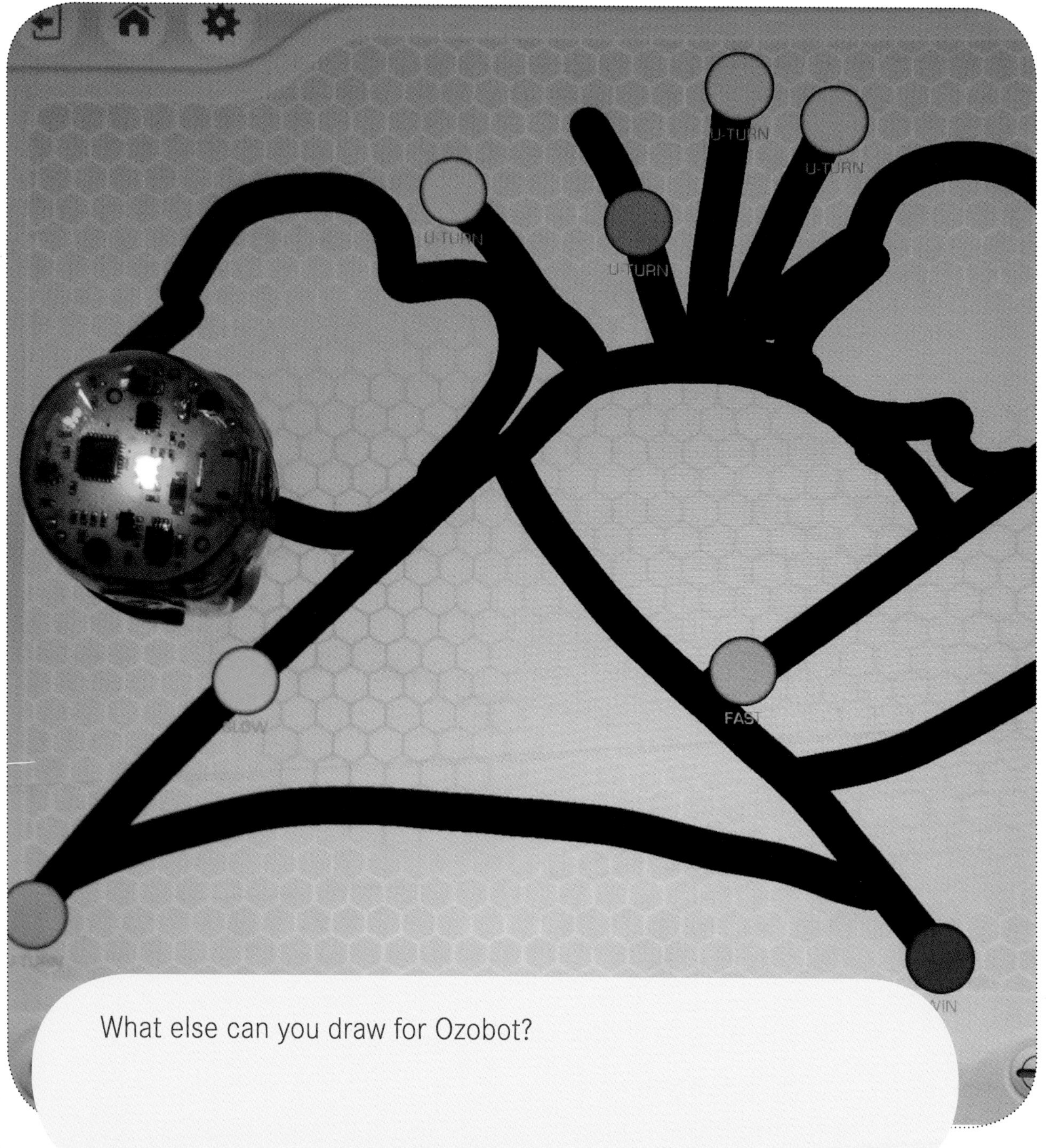

What else can you draw for Ozobot?

Explore with Ozobot

When Ozobot reaches a part of your neighborhood that is special, try using OzoCodes. For example, you can make Ozobot spin in front of your favorite places. Now watch and see which path Ozobot takes around your neighborhood!

Glossary

calibrate (KAL-uh-brayt) to adjust a device so it works correctly in different situations

code (KODE) ideas written using computer language

optical (AHP-ti-kuhl) having to do with sight

OzoCodes (OH-zoh-kohdz) special codes that Ozobot can read and understand

programs (PROH-gramz) sets of instructions for computers to follow

sensors (SEN-surz) electronic devices that can detect things such as light, color, or sound

Find Out More

Books

Benovich Gilby, Nancy. *FIRST Robotics*. Ann Arbor, MI: Cherry Lake Publishing, 2016.

Benson, Pete. *Scratch*. Ann Arbor, MI: Cherry Lake Publishing, 2016.

Roslund, Samantha, and Emily Puckett Rodgers. *Makerspaces*. Ann Arbor, MI: Cherry Lake Publishing, 2014.

Web Sites

OzoBlockly
www.ozoblockly.com
Use your computer to control Ozobot using OzoBlockly.

Ozobot
www.ozobot.com
Find lots of fun things to do with Ozobot on the Ozobot Web site.

YouTube—Ozobot
www.youtube.com/user/OZOBOT/videos
Watch videos and learn more about Ozobot.

Index

About the Author

Amber Lovett likes playing with robots and technology. She teaches science, technology, engineering, and math at a school in Arizona.